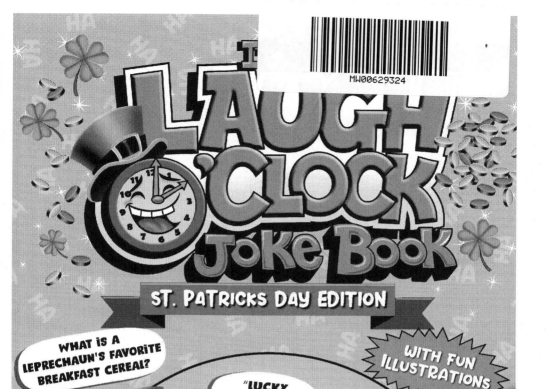

LAUGH O'CLOCK JOKE BOOK

ST. PATRICKS DAY EDITION

WHAT IS A LEPRECHAUN'S FAVORITE BREAKFAST CEREAL?

"LUCKY CHARMS."

WITH FUN ILLUSTRATIONS

RIDDLELAND

Table of Contents

Riddleland Bonus Book

FUN RIDDLES
AND
silly jokes
— FOR —
KIDS AND FAMILY

50 bonus
riddles, jokes and funny stories

RIDDLELAND

SCAN ME

http://pixelfy.me/riddlelandbonus

Thank you for buying this book. We would like to share a special bonus as a token of appreciation. It is a collection of 50 original jokes, riddles, and two super funny stories!

Join our **Facebook Group**
at **Riddleland for Kids** to get
daily jokes and riddles.

Introduction

"Life is filled with lots of things that make it all worthwhile, but none is better than your little smile."

Get ready to laugh! *It's Laugh O'Clock Joke Book: St Patrick's Day Edition* is different from other joke books. This book is not meant to be read alone - although it can be; instead it is a game to be played with siblings, friends, family or between two people to see who can make the other laugh first. It's time to laugh; it's always laugh o'clock somewhere.

These jokes are written to provide a fun, quality reading experience. Children learn best when they are playing; reading is fun when it is something one wants to read, and most children want to read jokes. Reading jokes will increase vocabulary and comprehension. Jokes also have many other benefits:

- **Bonding** – Sharing this book is an excellent way for parents and children to spend some quality time having fun, sharing laughs, and making memories.

- **Building Confidence** - When parents ask one of the jokes, it creates a safe environment for children to burst out answers even if they are incorrect.
  This helps children to develop self-confidence and self-expression.

- **Improve Vocabulary** – Jokes are a lot of fun, and that makes reading a lot of fun. Children will need to understand the words if they want to understand the jokes.

- **Enhancing Reading Comprehension** – Many children can read at a young age but may not understand the context of words in the sentences. Jokes, especially puns, can help develop children's interest to comprehend the context.

- **Developing Creativity** – Funny, creative jokes can help children develop their sense of humor while getting their brains working. Many times a word in a joke can be taken two ways, and picturing it both ways leads to creative imagery.

- **Developing Logical Thinking Skills** – Because many jokes have a dual play on words, children must use logic to decide which meaning the speaker intended.

 Enjoy the book, and, remember, it's always laugh o'clock somewhere.

Rules of the Game

The goal is to make your opponent laugh

- Face your opponent
  Stare at them!

- Make funny faces and noises to throw your opponent off

- **Take turns reading the jokes out loud to each other**

- When someone laughs, the other person wins a point

First person to get 5 points, is crowned the Champion!

FUN FACTS FOR ST PATRICK'S DAY

Do you know where in the world has the shortest St. Patrick's Day Parade?

It used to be a village in Ireland called Dripsey between two pubs; but now it's in Hot Springs, Arkansas, and the route is 98 feet.

Do you know what a Lobaircin is?

I bet you've heard of them. When it's translated from the Irish, it means 'small-bodied fellow' – does that translation help? A Lobaircin is another name for a Leprechaun.

CHAPTER 1

The Lucky Shamrock Challenge

"To succeed in life, you need three things: a wishbone, a backbone and a funny bone." ~ **Reba McEntire**

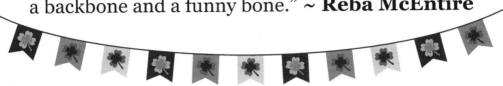

What do you call a leprechaun when he's in prison?

A lepre-con

How do you know when an Irishman is laughing?

He's Dublin over.

What do you say to a competitor in a St. Patrick's Day marathon?

"Irish you luck."

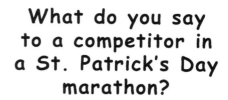

Why do leprechauns dance the jig so well, but their horses don't?

Their horses have two left feet.

What did the baby leprechaun find at the end of the rainbow?

A potty gold.

What does a leprechaun referee say at the end of a soccer match?

"Game clover."

What did the grass say to the leprechaun as he ran with joy?

"I am green . . . with envy."

Why would a leprechaun pick up plastic water bottles and old newspapers?

He's a wee-cycler.

What was St. Patrick's favorite type of music?

Shamrock and roll.

What is a leprechaun's favorite barbeque food?

Short rib.

What do leprechaun farmers grow?

Lepre-corn.

What did the leprechaun say at the stand-up comedy show?

"I'm greening from ear to ear."

What did one shamrock say to the other shamrock when he saw St. Patrick walking through the field?

"Look clover there"

Why would a leprechaun never tell a pig where his gold is hidden?

He is bound to squeal.

Why did the leprechaun wear a green dress shirt in the garden?

He was trying collared green.

What do you call a successful Irish farmer?

A man who is outstanding in his field.

What position does a leprechaun play on a baseball team?

Short-stop.

What is trivia about leprechauns called?

Little gnome facts.

What did the leprechaun call his rich elf cousin?

Welfy.

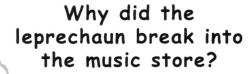

Why are leprechauns so concerned with global warming?

They're into green living.

Why did the leprechaun break into the music store?

He was looking for the lute.

What did the Irish dairy farmer give his cows to keep them busy?

He gave them some cattle-logs to read.

What do you call a leprechaun who paints forgeries of the rainbow?

A leprechaun artist.

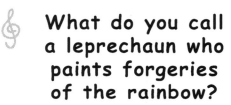

How is a device used by musicians to mark time like a leprechaun that lives in the city?

Both are metrognomes.

Did you hear about the medicine that St. Patrick invented?

They are anti-hisss-tamines.

What does a leprechaun use to buy snacks from a vending machine?

A lepre-coin.

Are rainbows fast?

They have flying colors.

What bow can't you tie?

A rainbow.

What did the shamrock say when he saw the four-leaf clover?

"That's unbe-leaf-able."

What do you say to someone who claims to see more than seven colors in a rainbow?

"That's just a pigment of your imagination."

How is a leprechaun saying, "Trust me" like a matador's cape?

Both are red flags.

What is green, has ten legs and no point?

A basketball team for leprechauns.

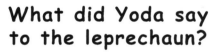

What did Yoda say to the leprechaun?

"Green and lucky I am, share your gold I can?"

Why did the leprechaun get jealous?

He caught his wife kissing the Blarney Stone.

Who is a leprechaun's favorite superhero?
The Green Lantern.

What sport do leprechauns like to play?

Rainbowling.

How do you talk to a leprechaun?

Use small words.

Why didn't the snake talk to St. Patrick?

It had a frog in its throat.

What does the four-leaf clover shout all day on St. Patrick's Day?

"Leaf me alone!"

What did the leprechaun do when he saw a sign in a store window that said, "Man Wanted for Gold Robbery"?

He went in and applied for the job.

How do you catch a lepre-con?

You send an under-clover police officer.

Why didn't the leprechaun eat lunch with his friends?

Because he already had a pot of gold before coming over!

Leprechauns enjoy playing their flutes and violins; how many songs should you request a leprechaun play for you?

Fortunes!

What does St. Patrick order at a seafood restaurant?

A sham rock lobster.

What do the leprechaun babies called their father?

Pop-chaun.

What do leprechauns call the meadows where they live?

Gnome man's land.

What do leprechauns and beer bottles have in common?

They are both empty above the neck.

Why did the leprechaun attend the Oscars?

He made the shortlist.

What did the police officer say when the waitress asked what he wanted to order at the cafe on St. Patrick's Day?

"Irish Stew in the name of the law."

What does an old leprechaun man sit in?

A shamrock-ing chair

What do you call something that will cheer up a sad leprechaun?

A pygmy up.

What did the leprechaun say when he walked into the cafe with a piece of asphalt under his arm?

"One lime milkshake, please, and one for the road."

What do ghosts drink on St. Patrick's Day?

Boo-s.

What did the leprechaun shout when teams were being picked?

"Pygmy; pygmy."

What is the leprechaun's secret stew ingredient?

A little bit of Gaelic.

How are Olympic athletes different from leprechauns and tanned models?

The athletes crave gold, silver, and bronze, but the leprechaun prefers gold and the tan model only thinks of bronze.

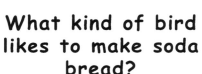

What kind of bird likes to make soda bread?

A dough-dough.

How does an Irish dairy farmer keep track of his cows?

With a cow-culator.

Why should you never own a wheelbarrow full of fourleaf clovers?

You will be pushing your luck.

Why didn't the leprechaun use a handkerchief when he sneezed?

He prefers mischief.

Why did the Irish farmer insist on growing both a green cabbage and a purple cabbage?

Because two heads are better than one.

What is St Patrick's favorite cake?
Paddy Cake.

What's better than change in the weather?

Gold coins at the end of the rainbow.

Are Irish cows and pigs funny?

Yes; the beef is corny and the pigs are big hams.

How is a recruiter like a cabbage farmer?

Both are headhunters.

What do you call a conversation between two leprechauns?

Small talk.

Why did the leprechaun have to work a desk job when he started with the police department?

He was too green for a patrol job.

What do you call an Irishman who cuts out the leprechaun from the Lucky Charms box?

A cereal offender.

Why didn't the Blarney Stone want to listen to his mum?

He was too hard-headed.

Why did the leprechaun queen go to the dentist?

To get her teeth crowned.

In what bank does the leprechaun hide his coins?

The river bank.

What do Irish pirates yell when they see the shore?

Ire Land ahoy!

How do you spot a jealous shamrock?

He's green with envy.

What did one plate say to the other plate at the St. Patrick's Day party?

"The Irish stew is on me."

How much did the neutron have to pay to get into the St. Patrick's Day party?

No charge.

Why did the boy plant the cabbage seed in the garden before anything else?

He wanted the cabbage to have a head start.

What did the Irish baker say when he found the soda bread dough he had lost?

"That's just what I kneaded!"

What do you call an Irishman that celebrates St. Patrick's Day all year round?

Evergreen.

How can you repair a dented head of cabbage?

With a cabbage patch.

Why are potatoes the best detectives?

They keep their eyes peeled.

What is a potato's favorite movie?

Silence of the Yams.

What do leprechauns do after school?

Gnome work.

What did St. Patrick say to himself when he stood in one place talking for so long that his cane took root and started to spout?

"The crowd isn't the only thing rooting for me."

Why is the Irish sheep dog so close to his owner's flock?

They have a very close relation-sheep.

What did St. Patrick say to the growths on his walking stick to determine if they were friendly?

"Are you my buds?"

What happened to the hot-tempered careless leprechaun when his friend gave him a brochure about an anger management class?

He lost it.

What do you call the doodles St. Patrick made in the dust with his walking cane?

Stick figures.

Why did the leprechaun's parents scream when the saw his grades?

It was full of bees.

Why did the Irish road get angry?

Someone crossed it.

What do Irish potatoes wear to bed?

Their yammies.

Why are most hot-tempered leprechauns employed as shoemakers and miners instead of doctors?

They tend to lose their patients easily.

What is the Irish trumpet player's favorite month of the year?

March.

Why did the leprechaun put his gold in the freezer?

He wanted some cold hard cash.

What happened when the businessman wished to the leprechaun that he could reach new heights?

The leprechaun turned him into a kite. (Remember, there is always a string attached when a leprechaun grants a wish.)

Most people focus on the clover's leaves, who focuses on the stem?

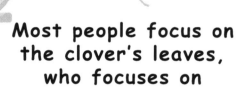

STEM educators. (STEM stands for Science, Technology, Engineering and Math.)

Why did the leprechaun have a nap under the trees?

It was a "for rest".

Why did the leprechaun go to the doctor?

He was feeling a little green.

Who is the first chauffeur in history?

St. Patrick; he drove the snakes out of Ireland.

Where are most
hot-tempered
leprechauns found?

Ire-land.

Why did the
leprechaun have to
take a ladder with
him to school?

It was high school.

What did they call
the news report
that described how
leprechauns could
run quickly but stop
instantly?

Braking news.

Can you describe the
flat, green grassland
that many leprechauns
live on in one word?

Plain.

How did the Irish
farmer fix his broken
coat?

With a cabbage patch.

How are shrimp and
a treasure-hoarding
leprechaun similar?

One is a shellfish and
the other is selfish.

  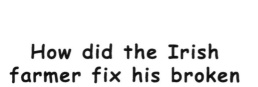

What did the Irish potato say to the soda bread?

"Would you stop loafing around already?"

Why are cabbages emotional?

They have a head and a heart.

Why did the Irish farmer go bald?

He developed a re-seed-ing hairline.

What happened when the shamrock was late for work?

His friends clovered for him.

Why did the leprechaun decide not to keep his secret gold stash at the bank?

There are too many tellers there.

What is a four-leaf clover's best friend?

A rose bud.

What's green and can fly?

A leprechaun in an airplane

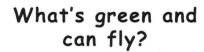

How do you get a tissue to dance an Irish jig?

You put some boogie in it.

Why was the three-leaf clover excited about the new year?

It was going to turn over a new leaf.

Which letter of the alphabet does the treasure-hoarding leprechaun like best?

"X"; because X marks the spot where the treasure is.

What ground-breaking invention do leprechauns find most fascinating?

The shovel.

What did the tree say to the four-leaf clover?

"I will be rooting for you."

What is the world's most colorful reptile?

A rain-boa constrictor.

What is it called when a leprechaun steals coins and hides them in the meadow, and then someone finds the leprechaun's treasure and takes it?

Giving him a taste of his own meadow sin.

Why did the leprechaun run away?

His feet couldn't reach the pedals to drive.

What do you get if Bambi crossed a rainbow?

A reindeer.

What is the Irish potato farmer's favorite day of the week?

Fry Day.

What's the difference between a strawberry farmer and a leprechaun?

One treasures his berries and the other buries his treasures.

FUN FACTS FOR ST PATRICK'S DAY

Have you ever heard someone shout 'Erin Go Bragh' at a St. Patrick's Day event?

If you have, over the years the words have become corrupted slightly from the Irish Eirinn go Brach, which means Ireland Forever!

Did you know that alcohol used to be banned on St. Patrick's Day?

Still up until the 1970s pubs were closed in Ireland on this day. However, nowadays, many people drink alcohol on St. Patrick's Day.

CHAPTER 2

Q&A Jokes

"A good friend is like a 4-leaf clover: hard to find & lucky to have!"

What is a leprechaun's favorite breakfast cereal?

Lucky charms.

What is a missing leprechaun called?

A lepre-gone.

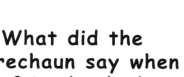

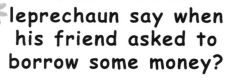

Why is a four-leaf clover like a best friend?

They are both hard to find and you're lucky if you have one.

What did the leprechaun say when his friend asked to borrow some money?

"Sorry I can't, I'm a little short."

Why should you never iron a four-leaf clover?

You wouldn't want to press your luck.

Why did the leprechaun become a landscaper?

He has green thumbs.

What does it mean when you find a horseshoe?

There's a barefoot horse somewhere.

Why do frogs love St. Patrick's Day?

They've always got a green outfit to wear.

How did the leprechaun astronaut get to the moon?

In a sham-rocket.

   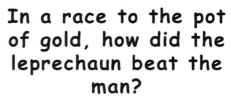

Why are leprechauns excellent secretaries?

They are very good at shorthand.

In a race to the pot of gold, how did the leprechaun beat the man?

By taking a shortcut.

Why would St. Patrick have chosen to drive out every snake that lived in Ireland?

Flying them was too expensive.

What job did the leprechaun lady do in the restaurant?

She was a short-order cook.

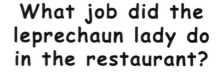

What does St. Patrick drink at a Chinese restaurant?

Green tea.

What did the Irish potato say to his girlfriend?

I only have eyes for you.

Why are leprechauns difficult to get along with?

They have short tempers.

Why did the leprechaun singer have to stand on a chair?

To reach the high notes.

Leprechauns are known for speed; therefore, if you are what you eat, where do leprechauns like to dine?

Fast food restaurants.

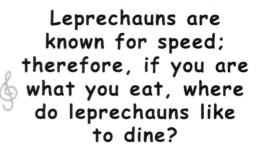

Why did the leprechaun lose the St. Patrick's Day marathon?

He did a jig instead of a jog.

Why can't you get leprechaun golfers to stop playing golf?

They don't want to leave the green.

Where do leprechauns play baseball?

Little League.

How did the Irish jig start?

Too much green apple juice and too few bathrooms.

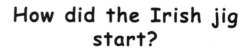

How did the Irish dairy farmer make milkshakes?

He put his cows on trampolines.

What do you call a fake diamond in Ireland?

A sham-rock.

What happens to a leprechaun if he falls into a river?

He get wet.

Why did the leprechaun end up in a mental hospital?

He had gone potty.

Why don't leprechauns tap dance?

They'll hurt themselves if they fall into the sink.

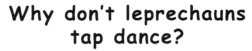

Why did the Irishman go sprinting down the road after speaking to his wife?

She told him that the refrigerator was running, and he was trying to catch it.

Why would the leprechaun cross the rainbow?

To make it to the other side.

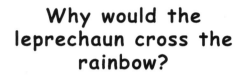

What do you call a short, sick Irishman?

A lepper-con.

What would you get if you were to cross a cowboy with a leprechaun?

A chili pot at the end of the rainbow.

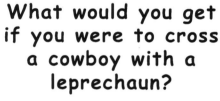

What do you call an Irish spider with long legs?

A paddy-long-legs.

What's purple and large and lives next door to Ireland?

Grape Britain.

What spells do leprechaun witches cast?

Lucky charms.

Where will you always find gold?

In the dictionary.

Why was the leprechaun on a mission to find gamma rays?

He wanted to look like the Hulk.

Why did the leprechaun keep a bottle of glass cleaner with him after two days of bad luck?

Because glass cleaner is supposed to stop bad streaks.

Why would a leprechaun refuse an offer of a bowl of soup?

He already had a pot of gold.

What is at the end of a rainbow?

The letter W.

What do you call a secret agent from Ireland?

Dublin 07.

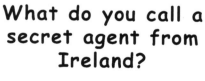

What happened when the Irishman dropped a tin of alphabet soup on the kitchen floor?

It spelled disaster.

What do you call an Irish jig if you do it at McDonald's?

A shamrock shake.

When does the leprechaun cross the road?

Only when it's green.

What does a leprechaun call a happy human wearing green?

The Jolly Green Giant.

What is the most environmentally friendly day of the year?

St. Patrick's Day because everyone is going green.

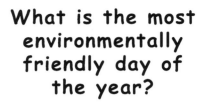

Why did the burglar break into the leprechaun's bathroom?

He heard he had a pot made of gold.

Why was the horse walking around in his socks?

He couldn't find his lucky shoes.

What would you get if you crossed a four-leaf clover and a chicken?

The cluck of the Irish.

What happens if you tease a leprechaun about his height?

He gets a little angry.

What do you get if you cross a frog with a leprechaun?

A little green guy with a croak full of gold.

Why do people wear shamrocks on St. Patrick's Day?

Regular rocks would be far too heavy.

What would you get if you crossed a four-leaf clover and a poison ivy plant?

A good luck rash.

Are U.S. leprechauns practical?

No; they thirst for gold and have no common cents.

How is an outlaw like a grocery-store cabbage?

Both have a price on their head.

How did the leprechaun justify flipping a gold coin when he couldn't decide between getting a haircut or reading a book?

Head or tale.

How does St. Patrick's Day always end?

With a "y"

How did the sportscaster describe the rookie leprechaun?

"They don't come any greener than this."

How are a psychic and a leprechaun with six shiny U.S. pennies alike?

The psychic has a sixth sense and the leprechaun has six cents.

What does a leprechaun girl wear in her hair?

A rain-bow.

What's long and green and full of potatoes?

A St. Patrick's Day parade.

Which country is closest to Ireland?

Iceland, it's only one C away.

What is the fastest growing country in the world?

Ireland—it's Dublin every day.

Why was the leprechaun balancing on a potato?

He didn't want to fall in the stew.

What happens if you cross a happy worm and a leprechaun?

You get a little green man squirming with delight.

How did the leprechaun make gold soup?

He put in 14 carrots.

What is a nuahcerpel?

It's a leprechaun running backwards!

Why can't you let Elsa from *Frozen* catch a leprechaun?

She will let it go.

What would a leprechaun say to the elf if he met one?

"What's the weather like up there, stretch?"

How do you know a leprechaun found a joke funny?

He's Dublin over laughing.

What inspires leprechauns to run so fast and race in the Olympics?

They crave gold.

Leprechauns prefer gold coins, but given a choice between U.S. coins or U.S. dollar bills, which would they likely choose?

The dollar bills because they are green.

What did the trickster leprechaun do when the greedy man wished for a million bucks?

Surrounded him with a million male deer.

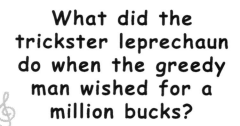

If you are Irish in the kitchen and Irish and in the living room, what are you in the bathroom?

European.

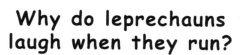

Why did the leprechaun hide behind a four-leaf clover?

He needed all the luck he could get.

Why do leprechauns laugh when they run?

The grass tickles their chins.

What is a liar's favorite place in Ireland?

The Blarney stone.

What is the luckiest crab in the world?
A horseshoe crab.

What is a leprechaun's idea of a balanced life?

A pot of gold in each hand.

Which weighs less, a pot of gold or a rainbow?

The rainbow is light.

Why would the leprechaun refuse to spell "part" backwards?

He knows it is a trap.

Which recent U.S. President is the Irish llama's favorite?

 President Barrack O'Llama.

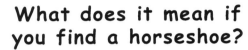

What is a leprechaun's favorite food?

Green eggs and ham with the eggs cooked clover easy.

What does it mean if you find a horseshoe?

That somewhere a horse is walking around with three shoes and just a sock.

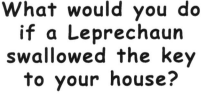

Why doesn't the bodybuilder celebrate St. Patrick's Day?

Every time he wears green people mistake him for the Hulk.

What would you do if a Leprechaun swallowed the key to your house?

Climb through the window.

What can stay in the corner but still go to Ireland?

A stamp.

Why did the shamrock go to the school nurse?

It was feeling green.

What is the leprechaun's favorite bird?

The golden eagle.

How many leprechauns would you need to screw in a lightbulb?

None. Leprechauns aren't afraid of the dark.

What is a leprechaun's favorite dog?

A golden retriever.

What do you call a mother leprechaun?

A mini-mum.

How can you honestly say someone who is one-percent Irish is just as Irish as a leprechaun?

Simple; "Both are wee Irish."

Do you know why we can't just assume that people use boring books to press four-leaf clovers?

Because you can't judge a book by its clover.

How did the clover patch feel after the long spring?

Re-leafed.

What is a leprechaun's favorite fish?
A goldfish.

Are rabbit's feet good luck?

The rabbit certainly gets a lot accomplished with them.

What happened when the four-leaf clover got stepped on and squished into the mud?

It made an impression.

Why did the superstitious man wear a fork prong around his neck?

It was the third prong, and the third tine is a charm.

How did the Irishman feel after flying in from Dublin?

His arms were very tired.

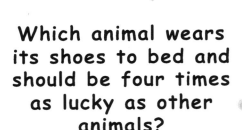

What kind of temper did the leprechaun have?

A short one.

Which animal wears its shoes to bed and should be four times as lucky as other animals?

The horse wears four horseshoes to bed.

What does St. Patrick and the shoe-making leprechaun have in common?

They both want to save your sole.

What is a leprechaun's favorite game?

Hide and Go-ld Seek.

Where do Irish sheep get their wool cut?

A baa-baa shop.

What do you call an Irishman who is mean to his wife?

A bachelor.

What is a cow's favorite holiday after St. Patrick's Day?

Moo Year's Eve.

Why did the leprechaun put his gold coins in the freezer?

He wanted cold, hard cash.

Why did the leprechaun cross the road twice and still find no gold?

He was double-crossed.

Why was the blacksmith so noisy making the lucky horseshoe?

He was doing a bang-up job.

What happened when St. Patrick told the snake he had to leave Ireland?

He became hiss-terical.

Why aren't there ever enough leprechauns to get the job done?

They are shorthanded.

What did the Irish dairy farmer say when all of his cows went on strike?

"This is udderly ridiculous!"

Why don't Irish eat snails like the French do?

They prefer fast food.

Why did the snake lose his case against St. Patrick?

He didn't have a leg to stand on.

What do leprechaun children have to do to make their parents happy?

Be good as gold.

How can you tell if the leprechaun's gold coin is new?

You can smell the mint.

Why did the Irish farmer plant cabbage?

He wanted to get ahead.

What did St. Patrick call his operation to rid Ireland of snakes?

Operation Scaling Back.

Why was the leprechaun not doing so well at school?

He was at the bottom of the class.

Leprechauns are amazing. Do you know why you need to hand it to leprechauns?

They're too short to reach it themselves.

Why did the leprechaun go to the bowling alley to find his missing hat?

It was a bowler.

What did the green hat say to the green scarf on St. Patrick's Day?

You hang around here. I will go on ahead.

Why bring a wheelbarrow when going searching for fourleaf clovers?

So if you find one you can push your luck.

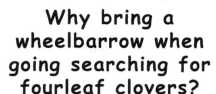

Why did the arguing couple visit the Blarney Stone?

Their marriage was on the rocks.

Was the Irish farmer discouraged when he only grew one head of cabbage?

No; he held his head high for all to see.

How does the leprechaun describe the grass stains on his pants from sliding in the grass?

Lucky streaks!

Where would you find a leprechaun with no legs?

Exactly where you left him.

FUN FACTS FOR ST PATRICK'S DAY

Do you know where the idea for Leprechauns originated?

It probably came from Celtic folktales of fairies who had magical powers. Typically, there were male cranky fairies who mended other fairies' shoes.

Do you know who Maewyn Succat is?

This is believed to be the name St. Patrick was born with. He changed his name to Patricius when he became a priest.

CHAPTER 3
Knock-Knock Jokes

"May your troubles be less and your blessings
be more, and nothing but happiness come
through your door." ~ Famous Irish saying

 Let's see who's at the door!

 KNOCK, KNOCK.

Who's there?

Warren.

Warren who?

Warren a green outfit today.

 KNOCK, KNOCK.

Who's there?

Erin.

Erin who?

**Erin really fast but still couldn't
catch that leprechaun.**

67

KNOCK, KNOCK.

Who's there?

Leprechaun.

Leprechaun who?

Lepre-con you out of your gold!

KNOCK, KNOCK.

Who's there?

Bee Leaf.

Bee Leaf who?

Bee Leaf in leprechaun magic on St. Patrick's Day.

KNOCK, KNOCK.

Who's there?

Justawee.

Justawee who?

Justawee joke is all!

KNOCK, KNOCK.

Who's there?

Potty.

Potty who?

Potty gold at the end of the rainbow.

KNOCK, KNOCK.
Who's there?
Irish stew.
Irish stew who?
As an officer of the law — Irish stew.

KNOCK, KNOCK.
Who's there?
Pat.
Pat who?
Pat your coat on; the St. Patrick's Day parade has already started.

KNOCK, KNOCK.
Who's there?
Saint.
Saint who?
Saint no time to be asking questions. Please open the door!

KNOCK, KNOCK.

Who's there?

Wendy.

Wendy who?

Wendy you think you'll be ready to go to the St. Patrick's Day party?

KNOCK, KNOCK.

Who's there?

Hayley.

Hayley who?

Hayley cab so I can go to the parade, please!

KNOCK, KNOCK.

Who's there?

Wayne.

Wayne who?

The Wayne-bow is out, come have a look.

KNOCK, KNOCK.
Who's there?
Garden.
Garden who?
Stop garden your gold and let me in.

KNOCK, KNOCK.
Who's there?
Collette.
Collette who?
Collette crazy, but I swear I just saw a leprechaun.

KNOCK, KNOCK.
Who's there?
Oscar.
Oscar who?
Oscar leprechaun where his gold is, and he will have to tell you.

KNOCK, KNOCK.

Who's there?

Juicy.

Juicy who?

Juicy any four-leaf clovers?

KNOCK, KNOCK.
Who's there?
Ireland.
Ireland who?
Ireland you some money, if you promise to pay it back.

KNOCK, KNOCK.
Who's there?
Seamus.
Seamus who?
Seamus open the door and find out.

KNOCK, KNOCK.
Who's there?
Irish.
Irish who?
Irish you would stop asking questions and just open up.

KNOCK, KNOCK.

Who's there?

Maud.

Maud who?

Maud as a hatter this leprechaun is!

KNOCK, KNOCK.

Who's there?

Mike.

Mike who?

Mike kind of town, Dublin is!

KNOCK, KNOCK.

Who's there?

Miners.

Miners who?

**Miners yours and yours is mine —
except for my leprechaun gold, that's
all mine!**

KNOCK, KNOCK.

Who's there?

Make Gnome A Steak.

Make Gnome A Steak who?

Make Gnome A Steak, leprechauns play tricks on people all the time.

KNOCK, KNOCK.

Who's there?

Don.

Don who?

Don go stealing my gold now, lass!

KNOCK, KNOCK.

Who's there?

Rain.

Rain who?

The rainbow that takes you to a pot of gold, that's who!

KNOCK, KNOCK.

Who's there?

Just ghost.

Just ghost who?

Just ghost to show you, leprechauns are real!

KNOCK, KNOCK.
Who's there?
Peas.
Peas who?
Peas tell me you're wearing green?

 KNOCK, KNOCK.
Who's there?
Shenan.
Shenan who?
Shenanigans are guaranteed if you open the door to a leprechaun!

 KNOCK, KNOCK.
Who's there?
Saint.
Saint who?
Saint a joke anymore, open the door!

KNOCK, KNOCK.

Who's there?

Watt Snoo.

Watt Snoo who?

Watt Snoo with you on this jolly St. Patrick's Day?

KNOCK, KNOCK.

Who's there?

Ha Pea.

Ha Pea who?

Ha Pea St. Patrick's Day.

KNOCK, KNOCK.

Who's there?

Gnome Eye.

Gnome Eye who?

Gnome Eye ABC's and 1,2,3s as well as my St. Patrick's lore; how about you?

KNOCK, KNOCK.

Who's there?

Bacon.

Bacon who?

I'm bacon a loaf of soda bread for St. Patrick's Day.

 KNOCK, KNOCK.

Who's there?

House.

House who?

House St. Patrick's Day going for you?

 KNOCK, KNOCK.

Who's there?

Fanny.

Fanny who?

Fanny one asks, I'm wearing green today, so don't pinch me!

KNOCK, KNOCK.
Who's there?
Orange.
Orange who?
Orange you coming to the St. Patrick's Day parade?

KNOCK, KNOCK.
Who's there?
Otis.
Otis who?
Otis is a great day for a rainbow and a pot of gold.

KNOCK, KNOCK.
Who's there?
Ida.
Ida who?
Ida want to tell you where my gold is!

KNOCK, KNOCK.

Who's there?

Minnie.

Minnie who?

Minnie are called but few are chosen to find that pot of all that is golden.

KNOCK, KNOCK.

Who's there?

Mister.

Mister who?

Mister rainbow by that much!

KNOCK, KNOCK.

Who's there?

Never-Never-Land.

Never-Never-Land who?

Never-Never-Land money to a stranger or believe a leprechaun when he says he doesn't have any gold.

KNOCK, KNOCK.

Who's there?

Needle.

Needle who?

Needle little help finding a leprechaun?

KNOCK, KNOCK.

Who's there?

Hannah.

Hannah who?

Hannah me some of that Irish stew, I'm hungry.

KNOCK, KNOCK.

Who's there?

Les.

Les who?

Les cut the small talk, leprechaun, and let me in.

KNOCK, KNOCK.

Who's there?

Nose.

Nose who?

I nose where the leprechaun's gold is hidden. If you let me in, I'll tell you.

KNOCK, KNOCK.

Who's there?

Gouda.

Gouda who?

Gouda luck finding that pot of gold!

KNOCK, KNOCK.

Who's there?

A herd.

A herd who?

A herd you were hiding a leprechaun in your house!

KNOCK, KNOCK.

Who's there?

Coleslaw.

Coleslaw who?

Coleslaw is like Murphy's law, except anything that can go right will go right.

KNOCK, KNOCK.
Who's there?
Gladys.
Gladys who?
Gladys St. Patrick's Day!

KNOCK, KNOCK.
Who's there?
A Parent.
A Parent who?
A Parent Lee it is getting close to St. Patrick's Day.

KNOCK, KNOCK.
Who's there?
Boy.
Boy who?
Boy I love St. Patrick's Day!

KNOCK, KNOCK.

Who's there?

Omelet.

Omelet who?

Omelet taller than most leprechauns!

KNOCK, KNOCK.

Who's there?

Pat.

Pat who?

Pat a smile on your face this St. Patrick's Day!

 KNOCK, KNOCK.

Who's there?

Robin.

Robin who?

Robin you leprechaun! Hand over your gold!

 KNOCK, KNOCK.

Who's there?

Noah.

Noah who?

Noah a place I can get some delicious Irish stew?

KNOCK, KNOCK.
Who's there?
Sombrero.
Sombrero who?
Sombrero-ver the rainbow is a pot of gold.

KNOCK, KNOCK.
Who's there?
Walter.
Walter who?
Walter you doing? You are not wearing green!

KNOCK, KNOCK.
Who's there?
Stopwatch.
Stopwatch who?
Stopwatch you are doing and go get us some green drinks.

Do you know where approximately 250,000 people march in a parade on St. Patrick's Day?

In New York City. The parade is not one that has floats or cars. It has been running since 1762, but was cancelled in 2020 due to Covid, and in 2021 there was a Virtual Parade.

Do you know what a Seamroy is?

It's the name that the Celts gave to the shamrock, a three-leaf clover. They viewed the plant as sacred, and it was thought to symbolize the arrival of spring.

Did you enjoy the book?

If you did, we are ecstatic. If not, please write your complaint to us and we will ensure we fix it.

If you're feeling generous, there is something important that you can help me with – tell other people that you enjoyed the book.

Ask a grown-up to write about it on Amazon. When they do, more people will find out about the book. It also lets Amazon know that we are making kids around the world laugh. Even a few words and ratings would go a long way.

If you have any ideas or jokes that you think are super funny, please let us know. We would love to hear from you. Our email address is - **riddleland@riddlelandforkids.com**

Riddleland Bonus Book

FUN RIDDLES
AND
silly jokes
— FOR —
KIDS AND FAMILY

50 bonus
riddles, jokes and funny stories

RIDDLELAND

SCAN ME

http://pixelfy.me/riddlelandbonus

Thank you for buying this book. We would like to share a special bonus as a token of appreciation. It is a collection of 50 original jokes, riddles, and two super funny stories!

Join our **Facebook Group**
at **Riddleland for Kids** to get
daily jokes and riddles.

Would you like your jokes and riddles to be featured in our next book?

We are having a contest to see who are the smartest or funniest boys and girls in the world! :

1) Creative and Challenging Riddles

2) Tickle Your Funny Bone Contest

Parents, please email us your child's "Original" Riddle or Joke and **he or she could win a Riddleland book and be featured in our next book.**

Here are the rules:

1) It must be challenging for the riddles and funny for the jokes!
2) It must be 100% original and not something from the Internet! It is easy to find out!
3) You can submit both jokes and riddles as they are 2 separate contests.
4) No help from the parents unless they are as funny as you.
5) Winners will be announced via email or our Facebook group – Riddleland for kids
6) Please also mention what book you purchased.
7) Email us at Riddleland@riddlelandforkids.com

Other Fun Books for Kids!

Riddles Series

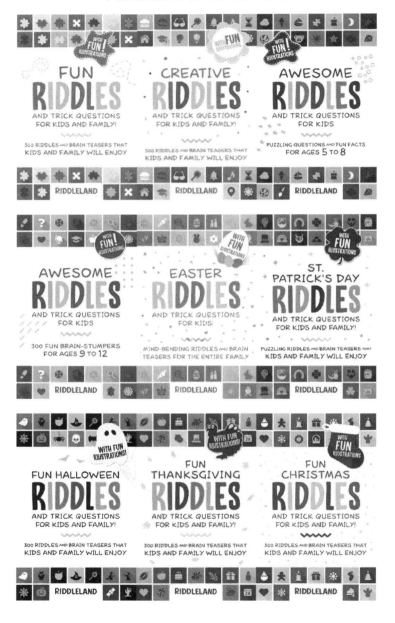

Riddleland

It's Laugh O'Clock Series

It's Laugh O'Clock
Would You Rather Series

Would You Rather Series

Get them on Amazon
or our website at www.riddlelandforkids.com

About Riddleland

Riddleland is a mom + dad run publishing company. We are passionate about creating fun and innovative books to help children develop their reading skills and fall in love with reading. If you have suggestions for us or want to work with us, shoot us an email at riddleland@riddlelandforkids.com

Our family's favorite quote:

"Creativity is an area in which younger people have a tremendous advantage since they have an endearing habit of always questioning past wisdom and authority."
~ Bill Hewlett

Made in the USA
Columbia, SC
22 February 2023

12814202R10054